It's Easy To Play Songs Of England, Scotland & Ireland.

Wise Publications
London/New York/Sydney

Exclusive Distributors:
Music Sales Limited
8/9 Frith Street, London, W1V 5TZ, England.
Music Sales Corporation
257 Park Avenue South, New York, N.Y. 10010, USA
Music Sales Pty. Limited
120 Rothschild Avenue, Rosebery, NSW 2018, Australia.

This book © Copyright 1982 by
Wise Publications
ISBN 0.7119.0178.3
Order No. AM31857

Art Direction by Mike Bell
Cover illustration by Mickey Finn
Music selected and arranged by Cyril Watters

Music Sales complete catalogue lists thousands
of titles and is free from your local music
book shop, or direct from Music Sales Limited.
Please send a cheque or Postal Order for £1.50 for postage to
Music Sales Limited, 8/9 Frith Street, London W1V 5TZ, England.

An Eriskay Love Lilt, 32
Annie Laurie, 21
Believe Me If All Those Endearing Young Charms, 34
Caller Herrin', 30
Charlie Is My Darling, 22
Cherry Ripe, 12
Cockles And Mussels, 36
Coming Through The Rye, 26
Danny Boy, 38
Eileen Alannah, 46
Galway Bay, 42
I Belong To Glasgow, 18
John Peel, 10
Killarney, 44
Lass Of Richmond Hill, 16
Little Brown Jug, 15
Loch Lomond, 27
Maybe It's Because I'm A Londoner, 6
Old Father Thames, 4
Roamin' In The Gloamin', 20
Rose Of Tralee, 40
Sally In Our Alley, 7
Skye Boat Song, 28
The Minstrel Boy, 33
There Is A Tavern, 8
Ye Banks And Braes, 24

Old Father Thames

Words by Raymond Wallace
Music by Betsy O'Hogan

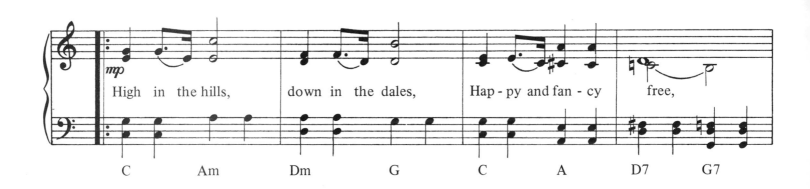

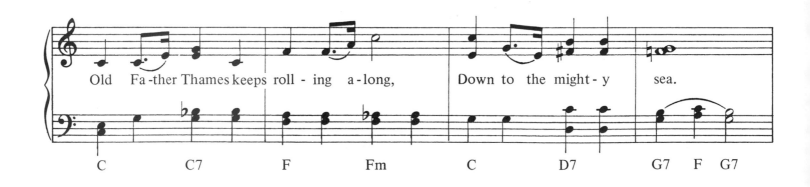

Maybe It's Because I'm A Londoner

Words and Music by Hubert Gregg

Sally In Our Alley

Traditional

There Is A Tavern

Traditional

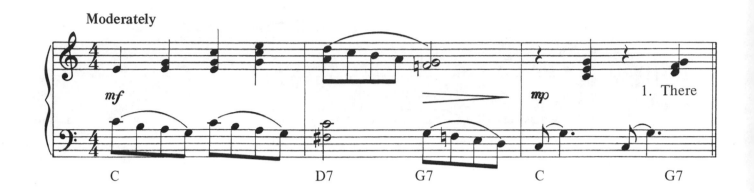

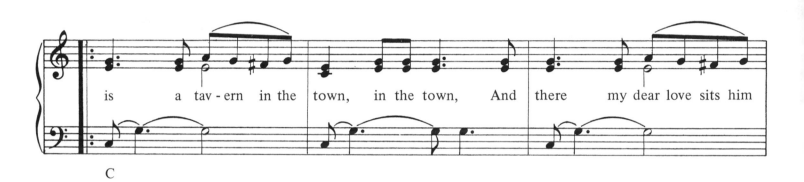

is a tav - ern in the town, in the town, And there my dear love sits him

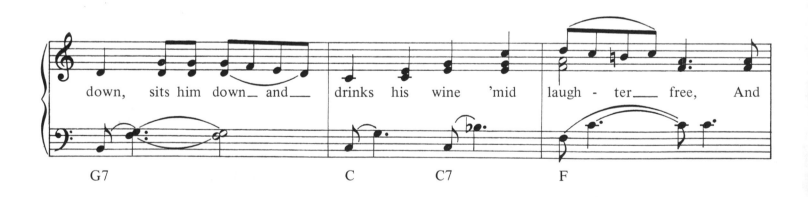

down, sits him down and drinks his wine 'mid laugh - ter free, And

nev - er, nev - er thinks of me. Fare thee well, for I must leave thee, Do not

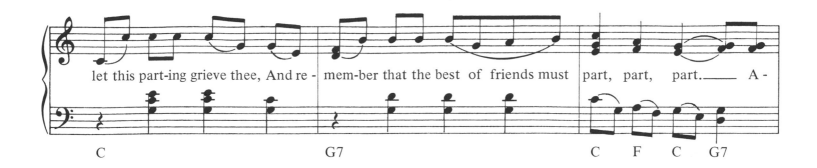

let this part-ing grieve thee, And re - mem-ber that the best of friends must part, part, part.____ A -

C · G7 · C F C G7

dieu, A-dieu kind friends a - dieu, a-dieu, a - dieu, I can no long-er stay with

C

you, stay with you____ I'll____ hang my harp on the weep-ing wil-low tree, And

G7 · C C7 · F

may the world go well with thee.____ 2. He thee.____

G7 · C G7 · C

2. He left me for a damsel dark,
   Each Friday night they used to spark,
   And now my love, once true to me,
   Takes that dark damsel on his knee.
        Fare thee well etc.

3. Oh! dig my grave both wide and deep,
   Put tombstones at my head and feet,
   And on my breast carve a turtle dove,
   To signify I died of love.
        Fare thee well etc.

John Peel

Traditional

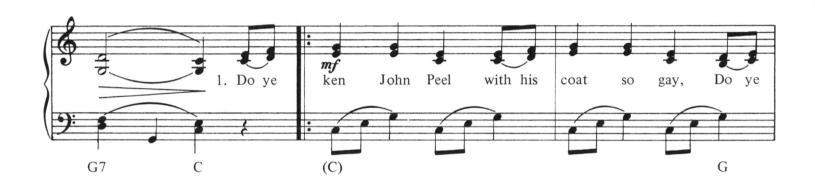

REFRAIN

sound of his horn brought me from my bed, And the cry of his hounds which he

(C)   Dm   G

oft - times led; Peel's tal - ly - ho would a - wak - en the dead, Or the

Dm   G   C   Am   F   C   A7

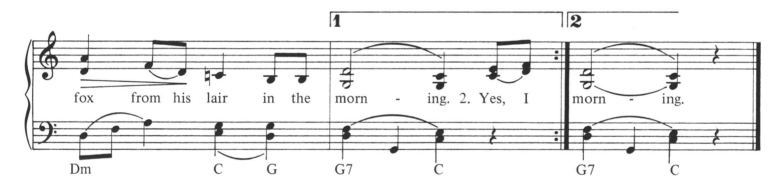

fox from his lair in the morn - ing. 2. Yes, I   morn - ing.

Dm   C   G   G7   C   G7   C

2. Yes, I ken John Peel and Ruby too,
Ranter and Ringwood, Bellman and True,
From a find to a check, from a check to a view,
From a view to a death in the morning.
For the sound *etc.*

3. Then here's to John Peel from my heart and soul,
Let's drink to his health, let's finish the bowl.
We'll follow John Peel through fair and thro' foul,
If we want a good hunt in the morning.
For the sound *etc.*

4. Do ye ken John Peel with his coat so gay?
He lived at Troutbeck once a day.
Now he has gone far, far, far away,
We shall ne'er hear his voice in the morning.
For the sound *etc.*

Cherry Ripe

Traditional

Rather slowly

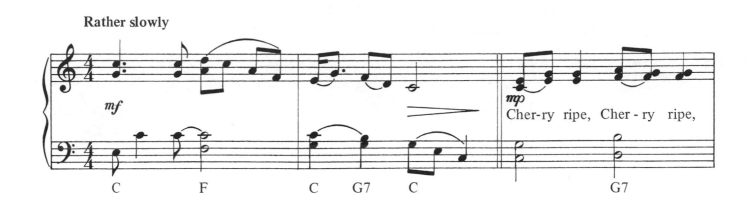

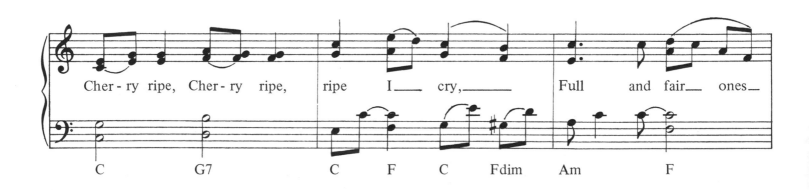

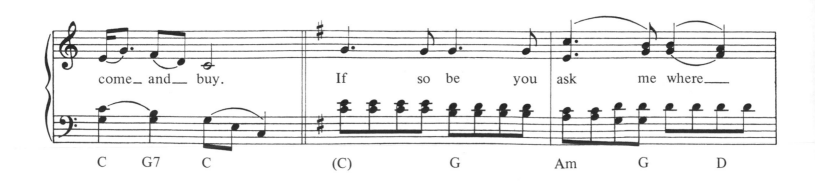

Little Brown Jug

Traditional

My wife and I live all a-lone In a lit-tle log hut we call our own.
My wife and I, we kiss and hug, And then we share that foam-ing jug.
I love my wife, in-deed I do, But lit-tle brown jug I love you too.

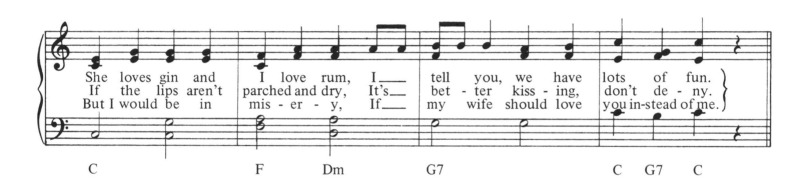

She loves gin and I love rum, I tell you, we have lots of fun.
If the lips aren't parched and dry, It's bet-ter kiss-ing, don't de-ny.
But I would be in mis-er-y, If my wife should love you in-stead of me.

REFRAIN

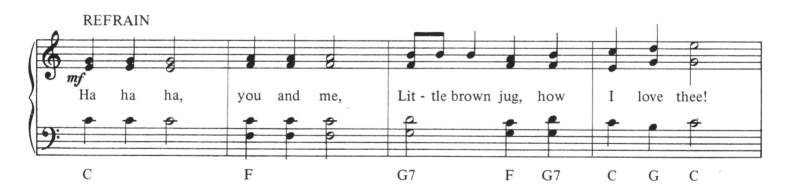

Ha ha ha, you and me, Lit-tle brown jug, how I love thee!

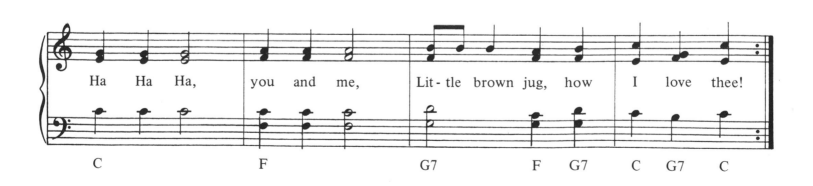

Ha Ha Ha, you and me, Lit-tle brown jug, how I love thee!

Lass Of Richmond Hill

Traditional

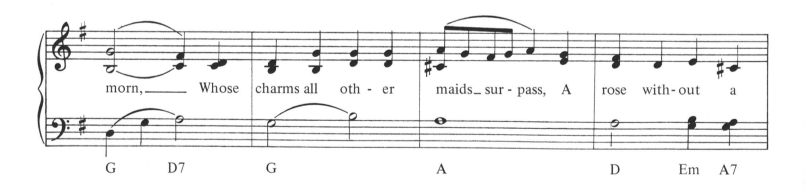

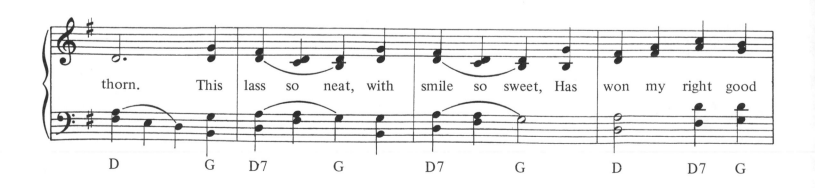

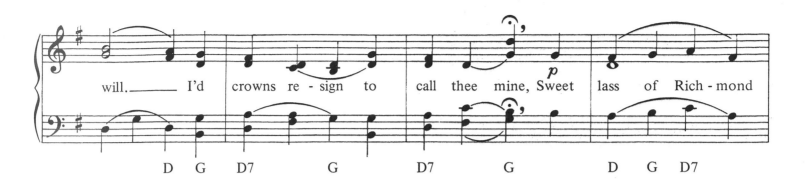

will._____ I'd crowns re-sign to call thee mine, Sweet lass of Rich-mond

D G D7 G D7 G D G D7

Hill._____ Sweet lass of Rich-mond Hill, Sweet lass of Rich-mond

G D

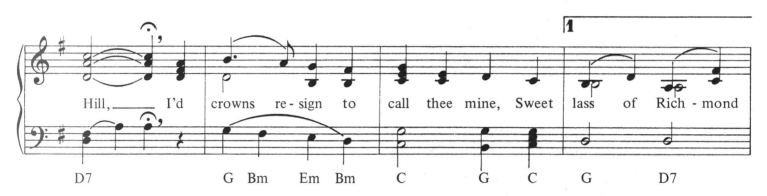

Hill,_____ I'd crowns re-sign to call thee mine, Sweet lass of Rich-mond

D7 G Bm Em Bm C G C G D7

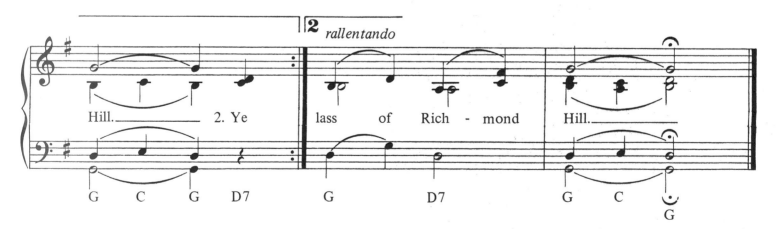

Hill._____ 2. Ye lass of Rich - mond Hill._____

G C G D7 G D7 G C G

2. Ye zephyrs gay that fan the air,
And wanton through the grove,
O whisper to my charming fair
"I die for her I love."
This lass so neat, with smile so sweet,
Has won my right good will.
I'd crowns resign to call her mine,
Sweet lass of Richmond Hill.
Sweet lass *etc.*

I Belong To Glasgow

Words and Music by Will Fyffe

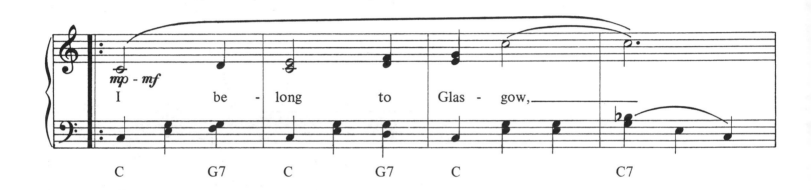

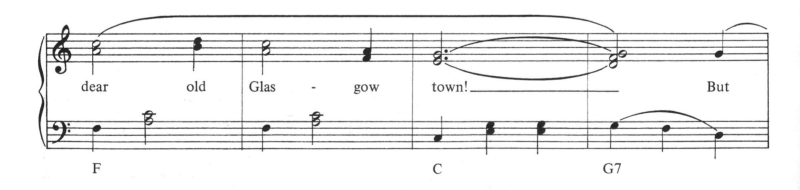

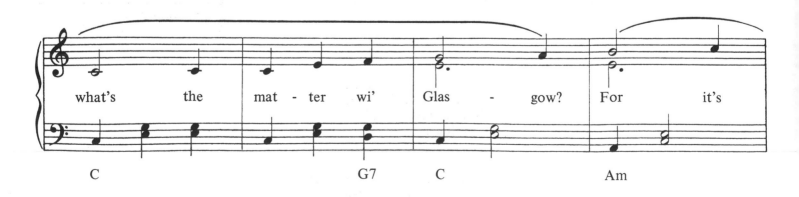

go - ing round and round._____ I'm on - ly a

D7　　　　　　　　　　　　　G　　D7　G　　　　C

com - mon old work - ing chap, As an - y -

D7　　　　　　　G7　　　　　F

one can see;_____ But when I get a

C　　　　　D7　　　　G7　　　　C

cou - ple of drinks on a Sat - ur - day, Glas - gow be -

F　　　　　C　　　　　F　C　　D7

longs to me.　　　　　　　　me.　　*ff*

G7　　　　C　　　　G7　　　C　　G7　　C

Roamin' In The Gloamin'

Words and Music by Harry Lauder

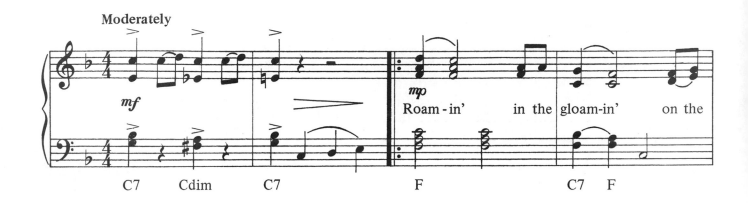

Roam-in' in the gloam-in' on the

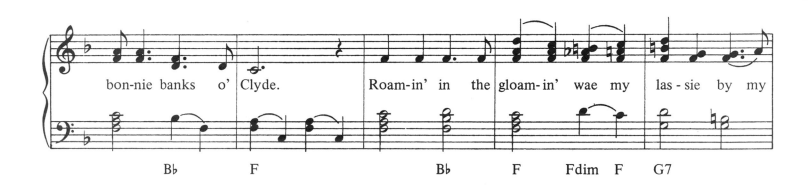

bon-nie banks o' Clyde. Roam-in' in the gloam-in' wae my las-sie by my

side. When the sun has gone to rest, That's the time that we love best.

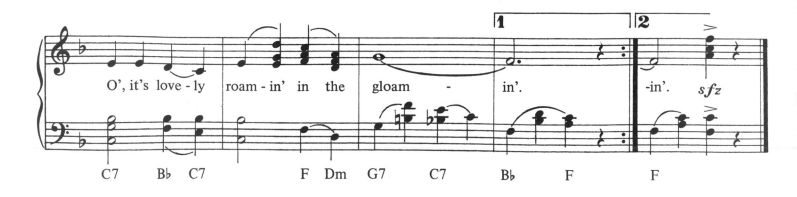

O', it's love-ly roam-in' in the gloam - in'. -in'.

Annie Laurie

Traditional

Moderately

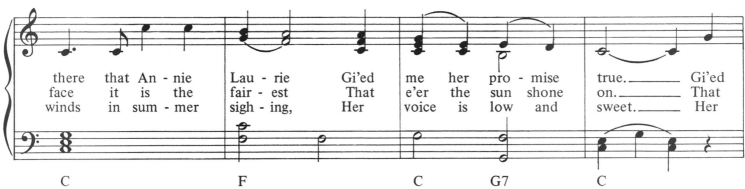

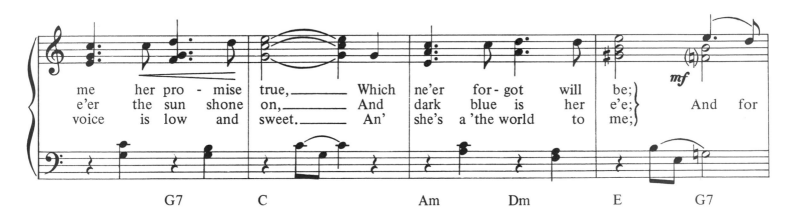

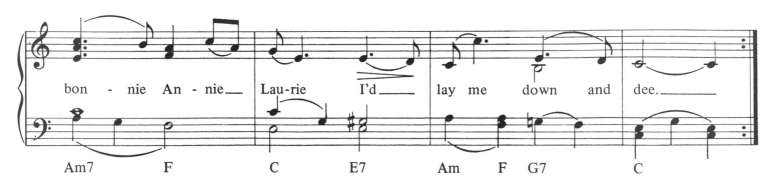

Charlie Is My Darling

Traditional

In march tempo

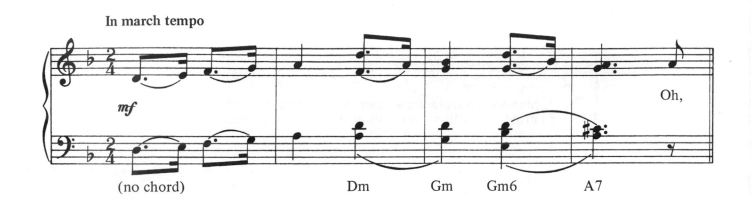

(no chord)   Dm   Gm Gm6   A7

Oh,

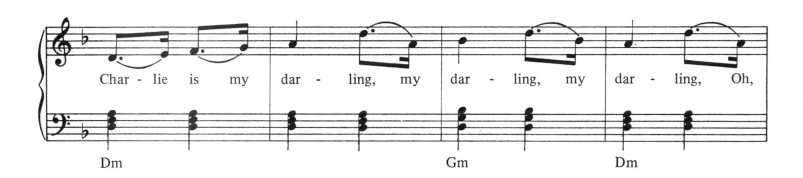

Char - lie is my dar - ling, my dar - ling, my dar - ling, Oh,

Dm   Gm   Dm

Char - lie is my dar - ling, The young Chev - a - lier. 1. 'Twas

Bb7   Dm   A7   Dm

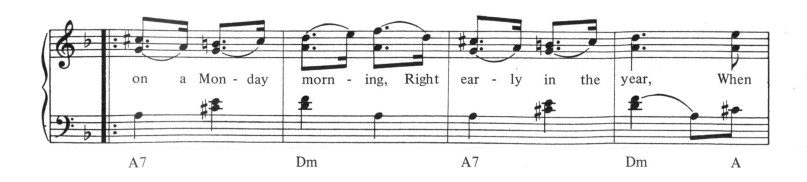

on a Mon - day morn - ing, Right ear - ly in the year, When

A7   Dm   A7   Dm A

Char - lie came to our___ town, The___ young___ Cav - a - lier, Oh!

Dm A Bb F Gm6 Dm A

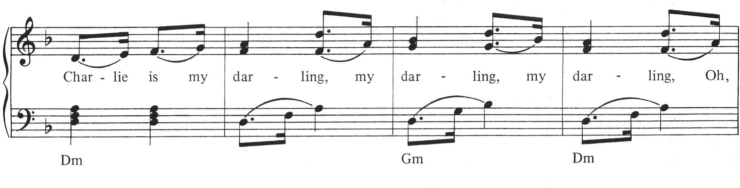

Char - lie is my dar - ling, my dar - ling, my dar - ling, Oh,

Dm Gm Dm

Char - lie is my dar - ling, the young Chev - a - lier. 2. As lier.

Dm7 Dm6 Bb7 Dm A7 Dm Dm

2. As he cam' marchin' up the street,
   The pipes played loud and clear.
   And a' the folk cam' rinnin' out
   To meet the Chevalier.
        Oh, Charlie *etc.*

3. Wi' Hieland bonnets on their heads,
   And claymores bright and clear;
   They cam' to fight for Scotland's right
   And the young Chevalier.
        Oh, Charlie *etc.*

4. They've left their bonnie Hieland hills,
   Their wives and bairnies dear,
   To draw the sword for Scotland's lord,
   The young Chevalier.
        Oh, Charlie *etc.*

Ye Banks And Braes

Traditional

25

Coming Through The Rye

Traditional

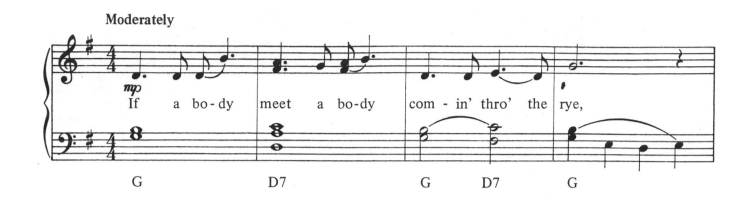

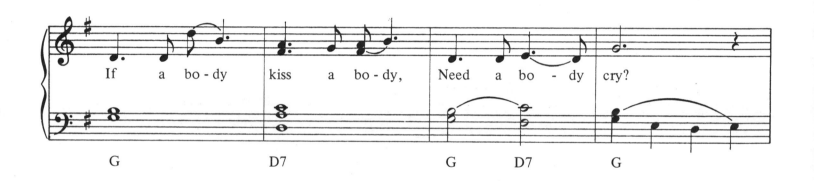

Loch Lomond

Traditional

Skye Boat Song

Traditional

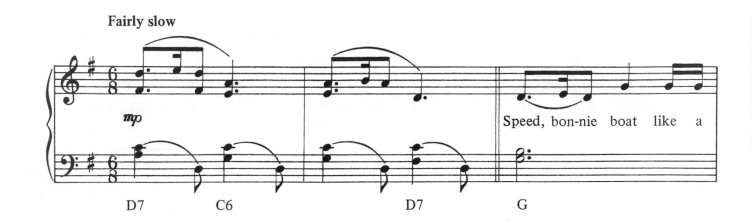

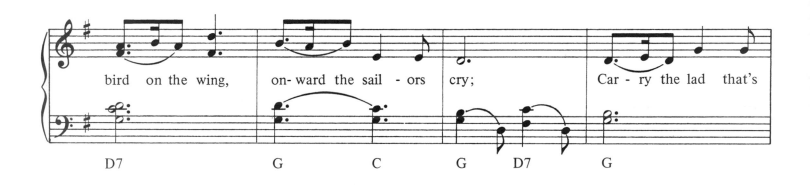

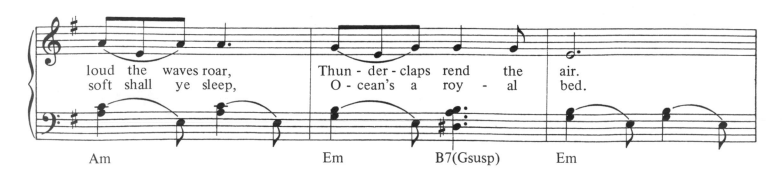

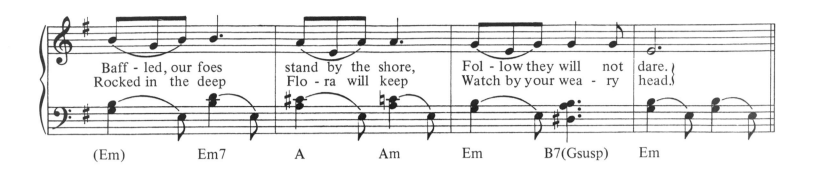

Baff - led, our foes stand by the shore, Fol - low they will not dare.
Rocked in the deep Flo - ra will keep Watch by your wea - ry head.

(Em)   Em7   A   Am   Em   B7(Gsusp)   Em

Speed, bon-nie boat like a bird on the wing, On - ward the sail - ors

G   Am7   D7   G   C

cry; Car - ry the lad that's born to be king,

G   D7   G   Am7   D7

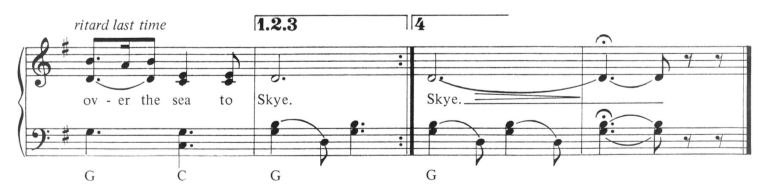

ritard last time   1.2.3   4

ov - er the sea to Skye.   Skye.

G   C   G   G

3. Many's the lad fought on that day,
   Well the claymore could wield.
   When the night came, silently lay
   Dead on Culloden's field.
        Speed, bonnie boat *etc.*

4. Burned are our homes, exile and death
   Scatter the loyal men.
   Yet ere the sword cool in the sheath,
   Charlie will come again.
        Speed, bonnie boat *etc.*

Caller Herrin'

Traditional

Fairly quick

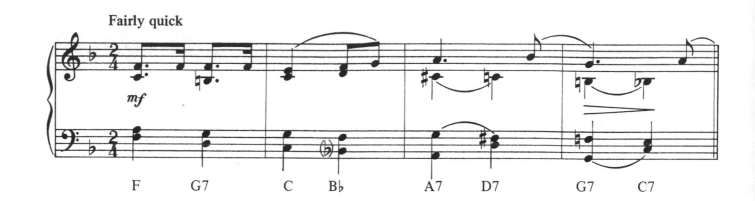

F   G7   C   Bb   A7   D7   G7   C7

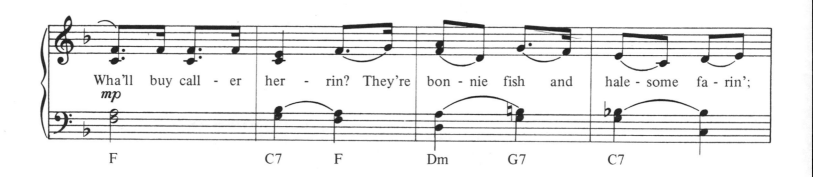

Wha'll buy call - er her - rin? They're bon - nie fish and hale - some fa - rin';

F   C7   F   Dm   G7   C7

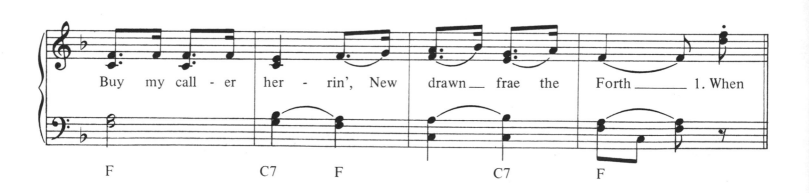

Buy my call - er her - rin', New drawn frae the Forth   1. When

F   C7   F   C7   F

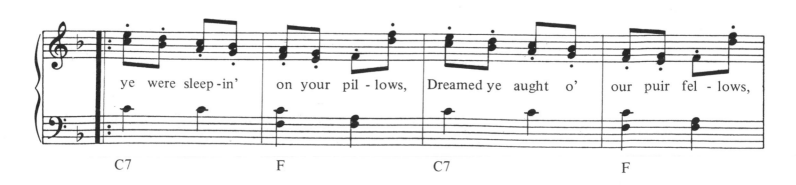

ye were sleep - in' on your pil - lows, Dreamed ye aught o' our puir fel - lows,

C7   F   C7   F

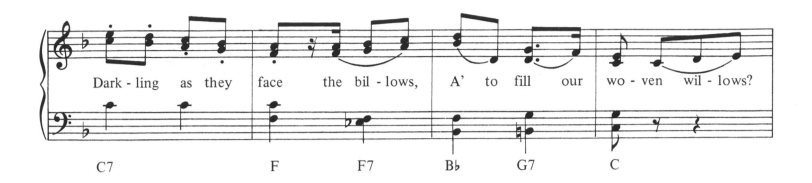

Dark - ling as they face the bil - lows, A' to fill our wo - ven wil - lows?

C7   F   F7   B♭   G7   C

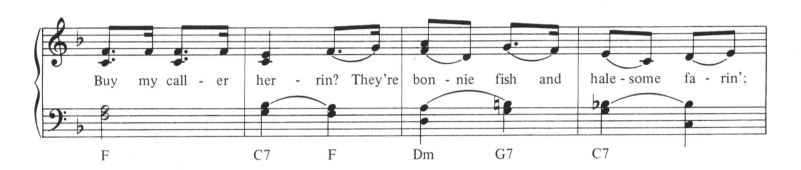

Buy my call - er her - rin? They're bon - nie fish and hale - some fa - rin';

F   C7   F   Dm   G7   C7

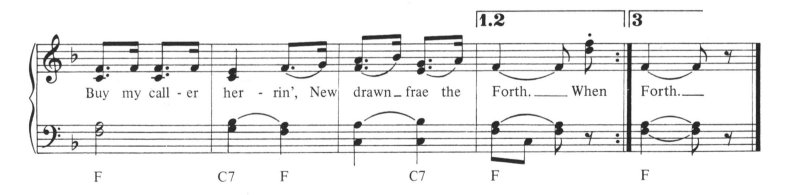

1.2 | **3**

Buy my call - er her - rin', New drawn frae the Forth. ___ When | Forth. ___

F   C7   F   C7   F   F

2. And when the creel o' herrin' passes,
    Ladies, clad in silks and laces,
    Gather in their braw pelisses,
    Toss their heads and screw their faces.
        Buy my caller *etc*.

3. Noo, neighbour wives, come heed my tellin',
    When the bonnie fish ye're sellin',
    At a word be aye your dealin',
    Truth will stand when a' things failin',
        Buy my caller *etc*.

An Eriskay Love Lilt

Words by Kenneth Macleod
Music by Marjory Kennedy-Fraser

Fairly slow

mp

F

1. When I'm

lone - ly, dear white heart,   Black the night   or wild the   sea,   By love's
mu - sic of my heart,   Harp of joy,   harp of my   heart.   Moon of

F

C7

light   my foot   finds,   The old   path - way to   thee.
gui - dance by   night,   Strength and   light   thou'rt to   me.

F   Bb   F

1

2. Thou'rt the

2

The Minstrel Boy

Traditional

Believe Me If All Those Endearing Young Charms

Traditional

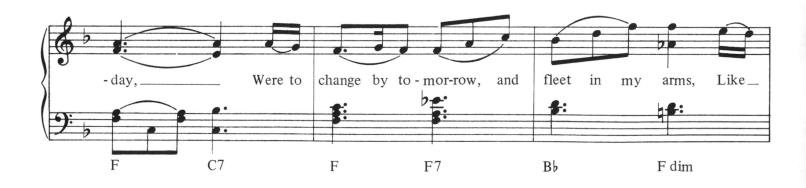

mo - ment then art, Let thy love - li-ness fade as it will;_____ And, a-

Bb   F   Bb6   A   C7

-round the dear ru - in, each wish of my heart would en - twine it - self ver - dant-ly

F   F7   Bb   F dim   F   C7

ritard.

still!_____ 2. It___ look which she turn'd when he rose._____

F   F   Dm6 C7   F

2.   It is not while beauty and youth are thine own,
     And thy cheeks unprofan'd by a tear;
     That the fervour and faith of a soul can be known,
     To which time will but make thee more dear!
     No, the heart that has truly lov'd never forgets,
     But as truly loves on to the close;
     As the sunflower turns on her god when he sets
     The same look which she turn'd when he rose.

Cockles And Mussels

Traditional

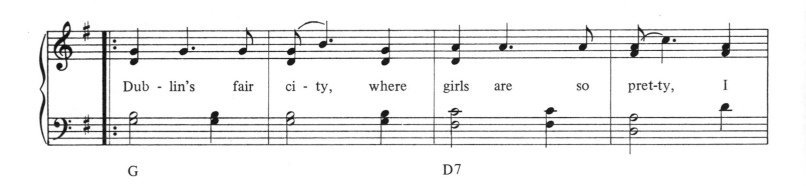

Dub - lin's fair ci - ty, where girls are so pret - ty, I

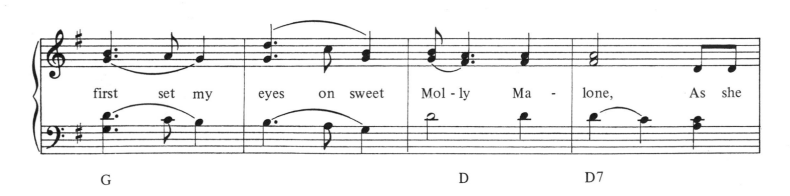

first set my eyes on sweet Mol - ly Ma - lone, As she

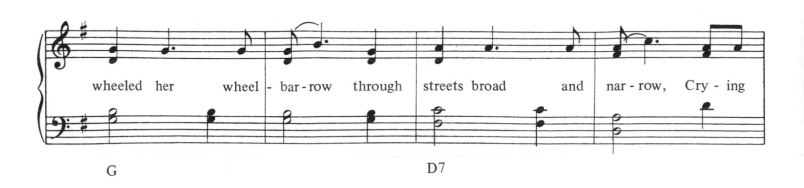

wheeled her wheel - bar - row through streets broad and nar - row, Cry - ing

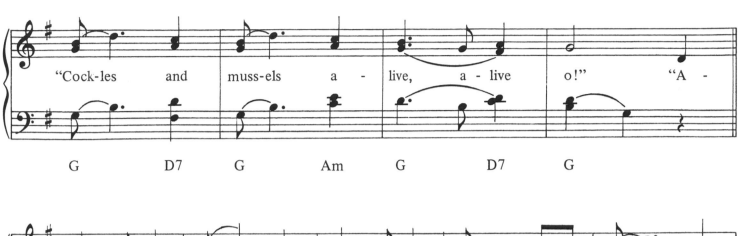

"Cock-les   and   muss-els   a - live,   a - live   o!"   "A -

G   D7   G   Am   G   D7   G

-live,   a - live   o!___   A - live,   a - live   o!"___   Cry - ing   "Cock-les   and

Em   C6   D7   G   D7

muss-els   a - live,   a - live   o!"   2. She   -live,   a - live   o!"

G   Am   G   D7   G   G   A9   D7   G

2.   She was a fishmonger, but sure 'twas no wonder,
      For so were her father and mother before;
      And they each wheeled their barrow through streets broad and narrow,
      Crying "Cockles and mussels alive, alive o!"

3.   She died of a fever, and no one could save her,
      And that was the end of sweet Molly Malone;
      Her ghost wheels her barrow through streets broad and narrow,
      Crying "Cockles and mussels alive, alive o!"

Danny Boy

Traditional

2. But when ye come and all the flowers are dying,
   If I am dead, as dead I well may be,
   Ye'll come and find the place where I am lying,
   And kneel and say an Ave there for me.
   And I shall hear, though soft you tread above me,
   And all my grave will warmer, sweeter be,
   For you will bend and tell me that you love me
   And I shall sleep in peace until you come to me.

Rose Of Tralee

Words by E. Spencer
Music by C. Glover
Arranged by H. Nicholls

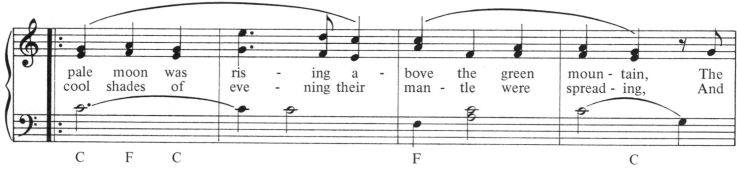

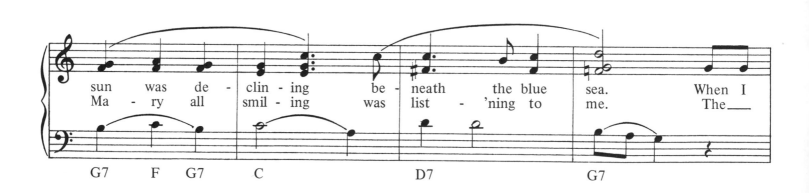

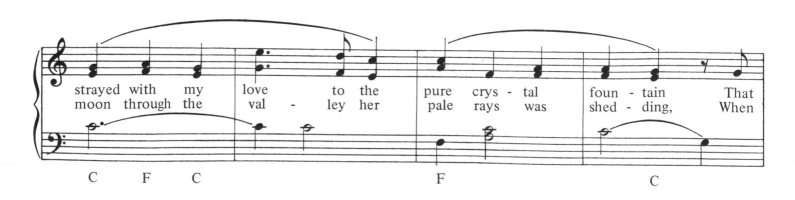

Galway Bay

Words and Music by Dr Arthur Colahan

trout stream, The wo-men in the mea-dows mak-ing hay,_____ And to
their way, They scorned us just for be-ing what we are,_____ But they

C7   F

sit be-side a turf fire in the cab-in, And watch the bare-foot Gos-soons at their
might as well go chas-ing af-ter moon-beams, Or light a pen-ny can-dle from a

Cm6   D7   G7   C7

play._____ 2. For the
star._____ 3. And if   there is going to be a life here- af-ter, And

F   Bb   F   Gm7   C7

some-how I am sure there's going to be, _____ I will ask my God to let me make my

F   Cm6   D7

hea-ven, In that dear land a-cross the I-rish Sea._____
                                              ritard.

G7   C7   F

43

Killarney

Traditional

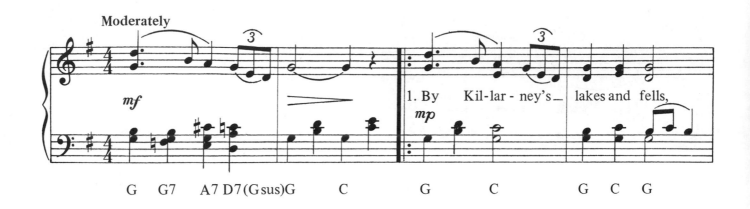

Moderately

mf / *mp*

1. By Kil-lar-ney's lakes and fells,

G G7 A7 D7 (Gsus) G C G C G C G

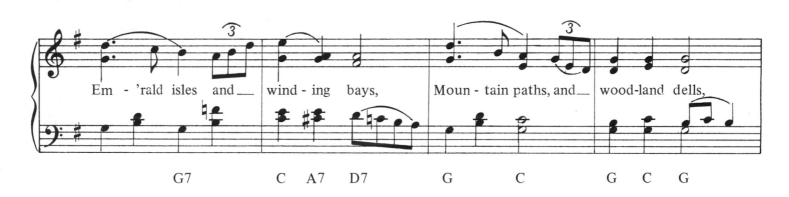

Em-'rald isles and wind-ing bays, Moun-tain paths, and wood-land dells,

G7 C A7 D7 G C G C G

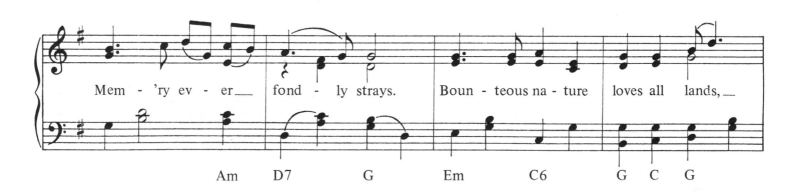

Mem-'ry ev-er fond-ly strays. Boun-teous na-ture loves all lands,

Am D7 G Em C6 G C G

Beau-ty wan-ders ev-'ry-where, Foot-prints leaves, on ma-ny strands,

E7 Am Em D C A9 G6 Am C dim Em G

2. No place else can charm the eye
   With such bright and varied tints,
   Ev'ry rock that you pass by
   Verdure broiders or besprints.
   Virgin there the green grass grows,
   Ev'ry morn springs natal day.
   Bright-hued berries daff the snows,
   Smiling Winter's frown away.
   Angels often pausing there
   Doubt if Eden were more fair,
   Beauty's home Killarney,
   Heaven's reflex, Killarney.

3. Music there for echo dwells,
   Makes each sound a harmony,
   Many voiced the chorus swells
   Till it faints in ecstasy.
   With the charming tints below
   Seems the heav'n above to vie,
   All rich colours that we know
   Tinge the cloud wreaths in that sky.
   Wings of angels so might shine
   Glancing back soft light divine,
   Beauty's home, Killarney,
   Heaven's reflex, Killarney.

Eileen Alannah

Traditional

The Beatles

Enya

Phil Collins

Van Morrison

Bob Dylan

Sting

Paul Simon

Tracy Chapman

Eric Clapton

Pink Floyd

New Kids On The Block

Bryan Adams

Tina Turner

Elton John

Bee Gees

Whitney Houston

AC/DC

Bringing you the words

All the latest in rock and pop. Plus the brightest and best in West End show scores. Music books for every instrument under the sun. And exciting new teach-yourself ideas like "Let's Play Keyboard" - in cassette/book packs, or on video. Available from all good music shops.

and music

Music Sales' complete catalogue lists thousands of titles and is available free from your local music shop, or direct from Music Sales Limited. Please send a cheque or postal order for £1.50 (for postage) to:

Music Sales Limited
Newmarket Road,
Bury St Edmunds,
Suffolk IP33 3YB

Buddy

Five Guys Named Moe

Les Misérables

West Side Story

Phantom Of The Opera

Show Boat

The Rocky Horror Show

Bringing you the world's best music.